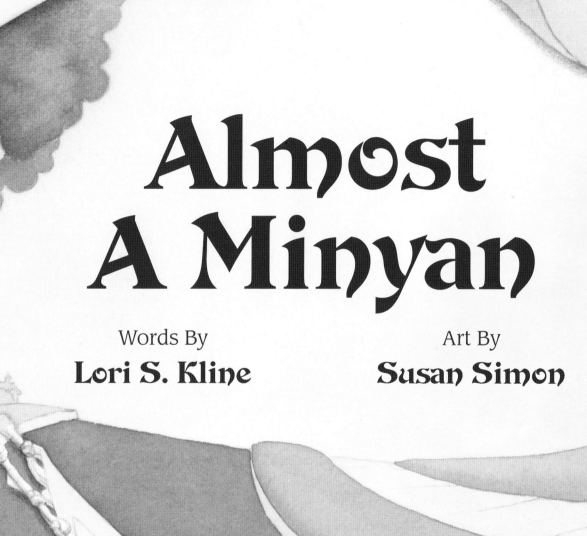

Almost
A Minyan

Words By
Lori S. Kline

Art By
Susan Simon

Other books by the author:
Josiah's Dreams

For reprint and bulk copy requests, contact:
Sociosights Press
1402 Crestwood Road
Austin, Texas 78722
512-789-5491
www.sociosights.com

ISBN: 978-0-9916327-4-9 (hard cover), 978-0-9916327-5-6 (ebook)

Printed in the United States of America

For Rabbi Jay David Sales:

my brother, mentor, and inspiration to find my voice in minyan.

—L.K.

To Ann Saalbach and Rabbi Joshua Lesser—my teachers;

and most of all and always, for Boyd.

—S.S.

My family lives two blocks from the shul

and mornings, at seven—it's almost a rule,

Papa arises and heads out the door

to daven, then kibitz, then head to his store.

He carries his tallis and tefillin together;

they're worn from his travels and all kinds of weather.

"One day you'll join me, with all my prayer gear."

Then gently, he adds, "The time's drawing near."

We live in a town that has just one shul

and even on Shabbos, it isn't quite full.

So mornings at seven, it's often the case,

there's almost a minyan—except for one face.

Or maybe it's two,

and sometimes, it's three.

In less than a year,

that face could be me!

You see, for a minyan, we have to have ten
adult Jewish folks who are women or men,
before we can say certain prayers from our siddur,
and when we get ten, well, Papa's eyes glitter.

For then we say prayers
like Kaddish and Bar'chu;
there must be a minyan
to read Torah, too.

So each morning at seven, he heads out the door

to daven, then kibitz, then head to his store.

He carries his tallis and tefillin together;

worn from his travels and all kinds of weather.

And sometimes I watch him

and fill up with glee,

quietly thinking,

"That tenth could be me!"

On weekdays it's hardest to get the full ten,

but Shabbos each week, they make minyan again.

For my Zayde stays with us each Friday night,

with kiddish and singing and food to delight.

Then off to the shul,

Zayde treks with my Father.

And though it gets dark,

both say it's no bother.

Two months ago, Shabbos,

my Zayde took ill.

And Papa stayed with him,

a whole week until

my Papa returned,

saying, "Zayde is gone."

"He lived a good life,

and now he's passed on."

All week people gathered at our house each night,
and we made a minyan by one candle's light.

And 'though every night, all ten made a minyan,

it didn't cheer Papa—in my opinion.

The next several weeks,

well, they seemed rather odd;

Papa would pass me,

and not even nod.

Each morning I noticed that

as he got dressed,

a small, torn black ribbon

was pinned to his vest.

Still, just before seven, he'd head out the door

to daven, then kibitz, then head to his store.

He carried his tallis and tefillin together,

worn from his travels and all kinds of weather.

And 'though he said nothing to me, (not out loud),

I think he felt better in prayer with that crowd.

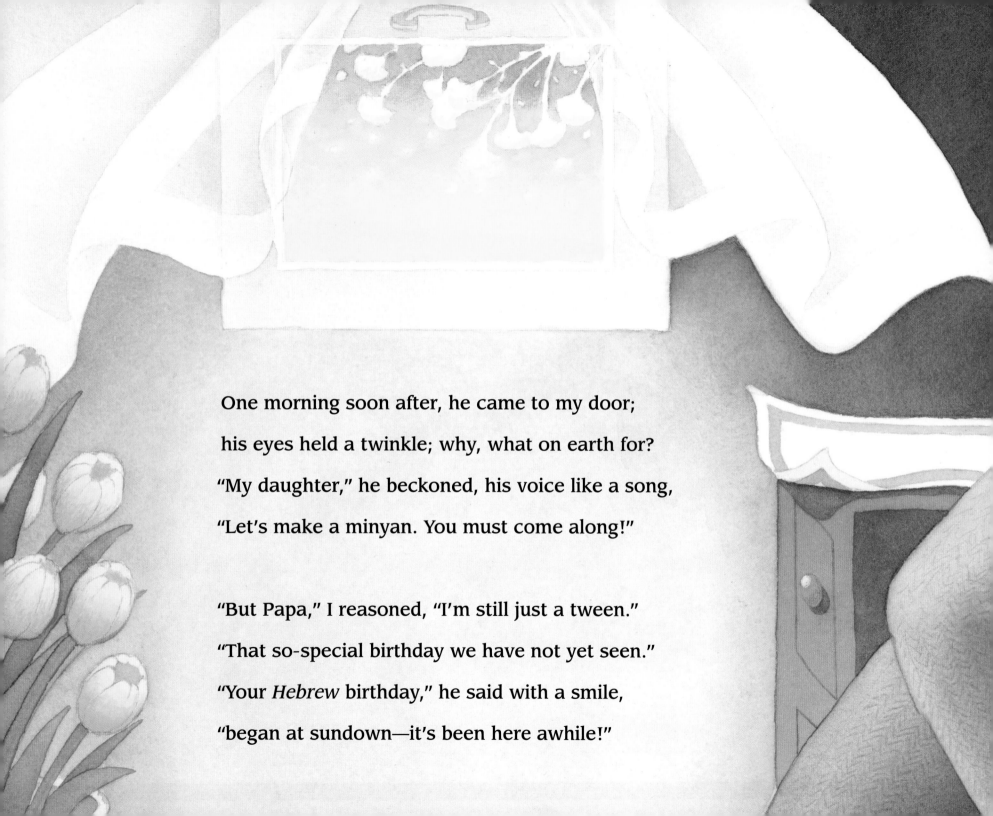

One morning soon after, he came to my door;

his eyes held a twinkle; why, what on earth for?

"My daughter," he beckoned, his voice like a song,

"Let's make a minyan. You must come along!"

"But Papa," I reasoned, "I'm still just a tween."

"That so-special birthday we have not yet seen."

"Your *Hebrew* birthday," he said with a smile,

"began at sundown—it's been here awhile!"

I jumped from my covers and scrambled to dress,

my thoughts were all jumbled, my hair was a mess!

I hustled to ready for what lay in store,

then Papa and I headed straight out the door.

But once at the shul, well, I became frantic.

I must admit, yes, I felt a bit panicked.

I hadn't the tallis or tefillin to don;

I felt almost naked; what would I put on?

I glanced all around me but hadn't a clue

then I looked to Papa, "What should I do?"

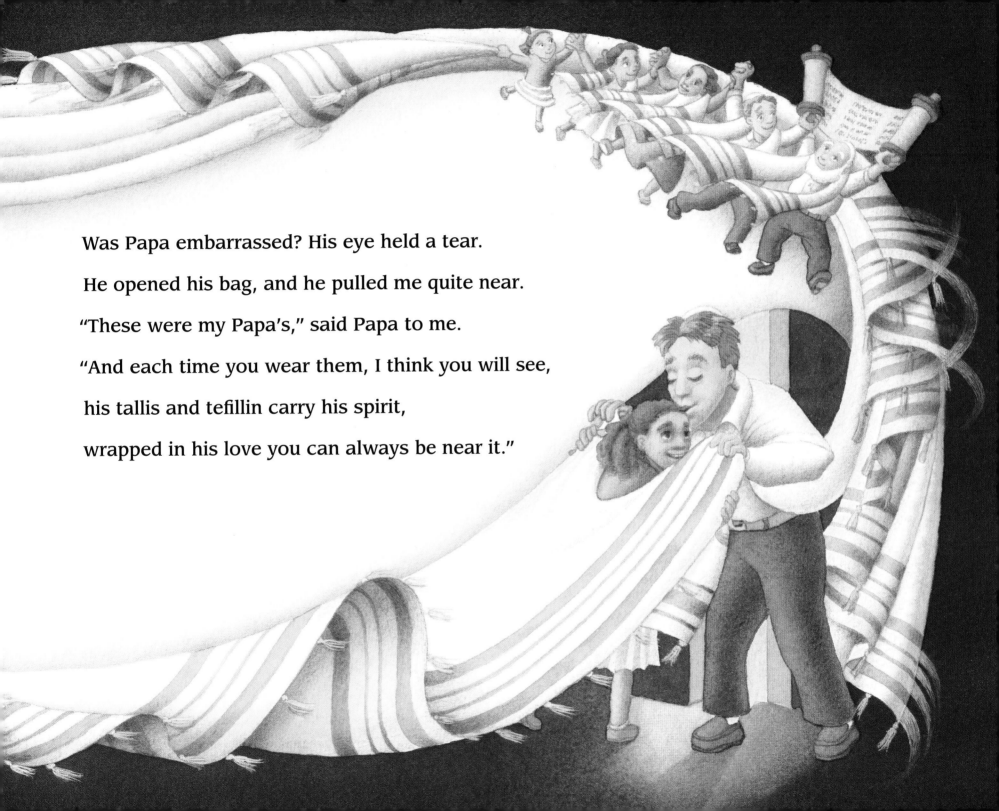

Was Papa embarrassed? His eye held a tear.

He opened his bag, and he pulled me quite near.

"These were my Papa's," said Papa to me.

"And each time you wear them, I think you will see,

his tallis and tefillin carry his spirit,

wrapped in his love you can always be near it."

And so we lay tefillin, my Papa and I.

At first it was tricky and I felt quite shy.

But once I was finished, I felt so connected
To Papa and Zayde and all they respected.

Papa smiled proudly—he teared up again.

Then, grinning, he told me, "Today, you make ten."

Glossary

Barchu: (Hebrew) the "call to worship" prayer in the morning service. "Barchu" literally means, "let us praise."

Daven: (Yiddish) to pray.

Hebrew birthday: The Jewish or Hebrew calendar is based on the lunar month. So the date a person is born, when calculated using the Hebrew calendar, fluctuates from year-to-year when compared to the Gregorian calendar.

Kaddish: (Hebrew/Yiddish) the prayer traditionally recited daily (for the span of 11 months) by individuals mourning the death of an immediate family member. This prayer exalts G-d's Presence in the Universe.

Kibitz: (Yiddish) to give unsolicited advice.

Kiddush: (Hebrew/Yiddish) the prayer recited over kosher wine. "Kiddush" comes from the same root as the word, "kaddish," meaning "holy." Traditionally, families recite the "kiddush" at home Friday evenings as part of welcoming the Sabbath.

Minyan: (Hebrew/Yiddish) a quorum; ten adult Jews over the age of thirteen, gathered for the purpose of prayer. Certain prayers and rituals can only be performed in the presence of a minyan.

Shabbos: (Yiddish) Sabbath, Shabbat. "Shabbos" has traditionally been a time for rest, prayer, study and family fun. The Jewish Sabbath begins at sundown Friday and ends at sunset Saturday when three stars are visible in the night sky.

Shul: (Yiddish) synagogue. A "shul" is the traditional place Jewish people gather to pray and meet as a community.

Siddur: (Hebrew) a Jewish prayer book. Literally translates to "order," as the prayers within all Jewish prayer books have traditionally followed a specifically prescribed sequence.

Tallis: (Yiddish) the Jewish prayer shawl, containing a long, knotted tassel at each of the four corners. The 613 individual knots in the tzitzis serve as a reminder of G-d's Commandments.

Tefillin: (Hebrew) a pair of black leather boxes slipped through straps. Each box contains four compartments with Hebrew biblical passages inside. One set is worn on the head and one on the arm.

Torah: (Hebrew) the Five Books of Moses written in Hebrew, on parchment, in scroll form.

Zayde: (Yiddish) Grandfather.

About the Author

Lori S.Kline lives in Austin, Texas with her husband and son. She regularly attends minyan at Congregation Agudas Achim, where she chants Torah and teaches Hebrew. Her first book, "Josiah's Dreams," was released in 2014.

About the Illustrator

Susan Simon lives in Tucson, Arizona with her husband and dogs. "Almost a Minyan" is her eighteenth children's book. In Judaism, the number "18" has a special significance and is the number assigned to the Hebrew word, "chai," which means "life." To see her other work, visit her website, www.susansimon.com.

About the Publisher

Debra L. Winegarten is an award-winning author and publisher. Her Hebrew name, "Devorah," means "honeybee," which explains how she gets so many things done. Learn more about her work here: www.sociosights.com and here: www.winegarten.com.